Cosmic Latte

ALSO BY EDWARD M. GEORGE
Midnight Coffee
Espresso Evenings

COSMIC LATTE

POEMS BY

EDWARD M. GEORGE

NEWSOUTH BOOKS
Montgomery

NewSouth Books
105 S. Court Street
Montgomery, AL 36104
www.newsouthbooks.com

ISBN-13: 978-1-60306-245-9
ISBN-10: 1-60306-245-9

Printed in the United States of America

To Sherry

Contents

Part III—Realities

Songs Not Sung

Alas for those that never sing,
But die with all their music in them.

— Oliver Wendell Holmes
from *The Voiceless*

For each of us there is a song
that lies within our souls
A song of life
that mostly goes unheard
among the clatter
of everyday living.

PART I— LOVE'S ILLUSIONS

Love is the state in which man sees things most widely different from what they are. The force of illusion reaches its zenith here, as likewise the sweetening and transfiguring power. When a man is in love he endures more than at other times; he submits to everything.

— FRIEDRICH NEITZSCHE

A Woman Looking
at the Night Sky

She said
You know it makes me feel
so small
when I look up there and
see all those stars
and think about how big
the universe is.

I looked at her ass
and thought
Well, I guess
it beats dieting.

Falling from Grace

Grace was my mentor
my guide
my engineer
on a long and magic trip
into the wonders
of her womanhood.

On the hilltop
we'd catch each morning's
orange sun sneaking
through the valley.

Her gentle knowing hands
led me
through each cold and moonless night
to where we'd dance enthusiastic
on dew-damp grass

Until we'd fall
breathless
to the earth
where she'd reach to pull
the first hint of sunlight
and then my sleepy face
to her breast

And slowly I would warm
and melt into
her essence

as she drew lines of love
upon my lips
and on my lids

And I would drift away
and dream of
an early morning hilltop
where Grace held my sleeping body
against her strong yet tender bosom
where I would drift away
and dream.

But then one morning
as the first light
sneaked through the tree tops
I left Grace
lying there
to greet the sun alone.

As I walked away
the breaking day
lit golden flames in her auburn hair
and drew against her flowing gown
a silhouette
of long familiar thighs.

She wiped her cheek
then slightly raised her hand
to wave good-bye.

And somehow we both knew
we'd never meet again.

Heliotropism

Heliotropism: phototropism in which
sunlight is the orienting stimulus.

— WEBSTER'S DICTIONARY

Her coconut-oiled skin
glistening golden brown
against the white beach.

She turns to catch the sun's rays.

I turn to catch hers.

Me and Lady Chatterley

Ah yes, to be passionate like a Bacchante,
like a Bacchanal fleeing through the woods,
to call on Iacchos, the bright phallus that
has no independent personality behind it,
but was pure god-servant to the woman!
      — LAWRENCE, *Lady Chatterley's Lover*

Her name was Anne
and she was cute
and seventeen.

One day on the bus to school
she handed me a book
and said Read this.

And being sixteen
and not too used to older women,
I said Okay.

That night I read and read
and have never since been
quite the same.

Of course, if I'd had any sense
I would have known
that this was not just literary sharing.

But being young
I returned the book
as ignorant as ever.

Love's Illusions

I've looked at love from both sides now
From in and out and still somehow
It's love's illusions I recall
I really don't know love at all.
   — JONI MITCHELL, FROM *Both Sides Now*

Why is it
that every woman I ever loved
broke my heart.

Even red-haired Penny
in the first grade
left me for the first guy
who had a Schwinn.

And then there was
red-haired Sarah
in junior high
who dumped me
when I got cut
from the football team.

And in high school
there was red-haired Randi
who dotted her "i" with
a little heart and
stomped on mine
when she wanted some "space."

(There was plenty
inside her head.)

And in my twenties
there was red-haired Sandi
who dotted her i with
a smiley face
but left me with
a frowny face.

Then in my thirties
there was red-haired Suzette
who was French
and hated all Americans
Me in particular.

And in my forties
I gave up
and married a brunette
who died her hair red
and took every thing I owned.

Thank You, Johnny Mathis

Chances are, cause I wear a silly grin
the moment you come into view . . .

Looking back
those had to be
the best of times.

A little Jack and Coke
and a lot of Johnny Mathis
on the stereo

And me and some flower
of young southern womanhood
dripping sweat on each others'
naked bodies
in that silly place
where you're not quite drunk
and not quite sober
and don't give a damn
about nothin.

First Love

First love is like a snowflake.
Like no other
and once it melts
It's gone
Never to be replaced.

Auld Acquaintance

New Year's Eve.
Almost midnight.
Another year
gone
without you.

Not just without you
but gone forever.
Another year
in both our lives
that we'll not have again.

What happened?
Is this pride's clever trick
on foolish lovers?

Words to Love By

Whatsa matta, boy?
an old man asked
as I sat mopey-faced
on a tree stump
near the sidewalk.

There's a girl
in my class.
I'm crazy bout her,
but she's a rich girl.
She don't know I exist.

He laid his hand
on my shoulder.
Boy, it's much better
to love a girl
you'll never have

Than to have one
you'll never love.
Believe me—
I know.

The Campfire

The campfire warms my brain
and I think of you,
the very you
I came here to forget.

The firewood crackles
and the smell
reminds me of those funny
French cigarettes
you thought were so
sophisticated.

A cool breeze comes along
and makes me think of sailing with you
off Cape Cod.

I lay back and
the big sky reminds me
of that chilly night we spent
watching the meteor shower,
you with your hands in my pockets.

And the moon,
of course the moon,
with the face that you said
was how we'd look
when we got old
together.

And then I close my damp eyes
to sleep
and dream of you.

Through with Love

She woke up crying.
She'd gone to bed crying.
She was through with love
      again.

What's the point anyway?
She thought.
I give and give and give
and every time
there's comes a day
I wake up crying.

It's better this way.
No make up.
No hair spray.
No shaving.
No more wondering if
my pubic hair is in
the latest fashion.

Who put men in charge, anyway?
God, what were you thinking?

The phone rang.
She quickly checked her makeup
as she reached to answer it.
It might be him.

Windows

We've been in love
for fifty years
he said
And I wouldn't change
a thing.

It's so good to know
that every time I look into
those green eyes I know so well
she still sees the young man
she fell in love with

And I still see
my teenage princess.

Nadine

Now, you got your Southern belles
and then there's Nadine.
Nadine wouldn't be caught dead
in a ball gown
or pretty much any other dress
unless it was for her own funeral.

Nadine's the kind of girl
who can speed shift a Camaro
or double-clutch a dump truck.

Whose idea of a square meal
is a baloney sandwich on white bread
with an RC
and a side of hoop cheese
and maybe a Moon Pie for desert.

Who knows a split-T
from a wishbone
and can throw a spiral thirty yards.

Who'll stay out till sunrise
at some joint
where they line dance
in work boots
and don't serve light beer.

Who wouldn't have a cell phone
and only turns on the TV
for Dale Junior or the Crimson Tide.

Who'll show up every day
for work at the plant
whether she's hung over
or still drunk
and put in a full day's work
without throwing up.

Who calls everybody honey
and tells you what she thinks
whether you want her to or not.

Who'll visit Hank's grave
every New Year's Eve
and toast him and Audrey
with Jack Daniels
and tell them how
Junior just don't get it.

Who says shee-it a lot
when she's mad
and when she's not.

Who'll go skinny dipping
in the creek with you
but won't let you
touch anything
unless she's in the mood
and there's a radio on.

Who sleeps on top of the sheets
in sweatpants
and a wore-out Lynard Skynard t-shirt.

Nadine, Nadine, the honky-tonk queen.
I guess she's just damn near perfect.

A Work of Art

Unlike all other pleasures, the pleasure we take in beauty is inexhaustible.

— Immanuel Kant

A beautiful woman
is like a work of art.
A miracle.
A gift.

Something to be appreciated again
and not always the same way

Each time you see her
from a different angle
or in a different light
or a different mood
or different dress.

Or with her hair a different way
or full of wind
or rain
or sun
or moon.

Or see her eyes
full of mirth
or mischief

or tears
or dreams.

Or feel her hand
or her heartbeat
or her presence
or absence.

A beautiful woman
is like a work of art.
A miracle.
A gift.

Turpentine and
Turkish Cigarettes

New York City—Summer 1958.
Her studio was on the second floor
of an old warehouse
around the corner
from Sal's deli where he worked
making deliveries on a blue bike
with a basket on the front.

Once in a while she'd order a ham and cheese
and a cream soda.
He'd make the delivery
up the dark creaky stairs
to the red metal door
with the sign that said "Art by Paula."

She'd always greet him with a smile
in her paint-stained t-shirt and jeans
and when she opened the door
there was always the smell
of turpentine and Turkish cigarettes.

She was about thirty-five
with black hair and pale skin—
pretty in a bohemian sort of way.
She painted abstracts for art's sake
and portraits to pay the bills.

He was seventeen and wide-eyed innocent.
He day-dreamed about her every day—
his day dreams smelled of her perfume
and turpentine and Turkish cigarettes.

One day hers was his last delivery of the day
and she said can't you stay a while.
He stayed that day
and often that summer.

She'd give him wine and Turkish cigarettes
and teach him about art and music
and life and love
and talk about Paris where the real artists lived.

His family moved to Michigan that fall.
He wrote for a while.
She never wrote back.

Years later
back in New York
he dropped by the deli to see Sal
who told him that she'd gone to Paris
about two years before.

Later that day he walked up the dark creaky stairs
to the red metal door.
There was still the faith scent of
of turpentine and Turkish cigarettes.

Lost Love

They say
it's better to have loved and lost
than never to have loved at all.

But true love
can never really be lost
or die
or hide away.
It's always there
right on the tip of your heart.

Always You

Don't ever let me catch you faking it,
making it up as you go along.
Don't ever let me catch you singing
the words to someone else's song.

No matter how tempting it may be
to blindly go as others do
remember that why I love you so
is that you're always you.

PART II— LIFE'S ILLUSIONS

This whole creation is essentially subjective, and the dream is the theater where the dreamer is at once the scene, actor, prompter, stage manager, author, audience, and critic.

— C. G. JUNG

Cosmic Latte

They tell me that
the universe
is the color of latte,
which I think is just fine.

Because it's only on
those sleepless nights
of just me and
an endless cup of coffee
that I take the time
to try to contemplate
Infinity.

Confluences

When Slim played the guitar
you could smell the whiskey
on his soul.

Each note cried like a baby orphan
as he played the country blues
And his gravel voice told tales
of wine, women, and woe.

Thirty years on a prison farm
left him permanently incarcerated
even with a pardon from the governor
who used to hang out in backwater joints
with his cheap mistresses
and bad habits

Where he'd listen to Slim
till daylight
when they'd roll him up
into a State limousine
that would deliver him
to the mansion

While Slim and a fifth of Jim Beam
hitched a ride with a waitress
to his rented trailer
on the back edge
of a cotton field.

On Meeting Jessica Lynch

She was a tiny thing
this first hero of the
War in Iraq
and looked a little confused
at all the clamor.

She tried to tell us
who the real heroes were,
but we wouldn't hear the truth
over the din that we'd created.

Unnecessary Complications

He was nineteen
and slender and firm
like a dancer.
She was seventeen
and sweet like
homemade ice cream.

They'd been in love
forever
and never known the touch
of anyone else.

Then came the war
and they were disconnected
for the first time.

He wound up
hauling a rocket launcher
through the desert
Dodging snipers
and IEDs
Losing his mind
a little at a time.

Then one day
he was on her front porch
Knocking on the familiar door

looking forward to her
helping him put back together
the pieces of his thoughts.

Not knowing that
for months
she'd had demons of her own.

First feeling guilty
for giving in to temptation
and then hoping to hear
that he'd died in the desert
so as to rid her life
of unnecessary complications.

The Sniper

Looking through a window
from the third floor
of a bombed-out building
He eyes his target
a thousand yards away.

Through his spy glass
he sees laughing
the man whose life
he will soon end
with a squeeze of a trigger.

This far away
he won't hear
the flesh ripping
or the blood spattering
against the wall.

Calmly.
Expressionless.
He lines the crosshairs
and slowly squeezes.
The rifle jumps
and he sees his target slump.

He Was a Soldier

He was a soldier.
Not a hero
just a teenage
moving target
with an itchy trigger finger
and a heart beating a thousand miles an hour.

He had no idea where he was
or why he was there.
He only knew he'd rather be
anywhere else.

But somewhere in his core
he knew there was a reason for all this
and there were people
who needed for him
to keep from giving in
to the insanity of it all.

He had walked through the looking glass
where without a second thought
he would give his life
to save a fellow soldier
whose name he didn't even know.

In his pocket was her last letter.
She couldn't take it any more.
She could never understand
he was a soldier.

Dogs I Never Had

There was something in the very air
of a small town in the Deep South then,
something spooked-up and romantic,
which did funny things to the imagination of its
bright and resourceful boys.
— FROM *My Dog Skip* BY WILLIE MORRIS

With so many little mouths to feed
and so little coming in
We never had a dog
when I was young.

Except that sometimes
in my fertile mind
with eyes shut tight
I'd play with an
imaginary canine friend.

Sometimes a collie like Lassie
would race gracefully across my mind
Sleek coat glistering
and she would tug on my sleeve
and pull me to where
I'd reach deep into an abandoned well
and scoop a two-year-old
from certain death.

Other days a sturdy shepherd
like Rin Tin Tin
would bound into my dream

And we would
throw our bodies
into the unsuspecting knees
of escaping bank robbers

Who'd go sliding
face first
into the street
where we would lift their guns
from stunned hands
and hold them
for the FBI.

Then there were days when
struck down by spring fever
I would only want to lay
in a shaft of sunlight
on the front porch
next to an old yeller mutt
who would lick my hand
in dog love,
selfless, unconditional
Dog Love.

At other times
I'd crave a smart dog
like Nick and Nora's Asta.

Or I'd wrap my thoughts around
a big brave St. Bernard
who'd look out for me
and rescue wandering little brothers.

Looking back
It may not have been so bad
that I was not confined to just one
living, breathing dog.

For if I had
I'd surely not have been so free
To dream those dreams
of mystic, mythic dogs
that even now
I still hold dear
For the light they brought
into the meager life
of a little boy
on a rickety porch
on a dusty gravel street.

Dreams

I have a dream . . .

— Martin Luther King, Jr.

Some people wonder
why in this land of dreams
and promises
So many go hungry
or sick
or ignorant
or poor.

But I wonder
how it would be
to have food
and medicine
and schools
and a little money

But no dreams
or promises.

I guess it would be a lot like
France.

The End of the Rainbow

I do set my bow in the cloud,
and it shall be for a token of
a covenant between me and the earth.

— GENESIS 9:13

They were three sisters
of the Great Depression
living on a farm in Elmore County
when, after a soft spring rain,
they saw the end of a beautiful rainbow
set down in their front yard.

Knowing for sure
that a pot of gold
would soon burst their chains
of poverty,
They leapt from the porch
and ran for a shovel.

When the first hole they dug
uncovered no gold,
they dug another
And another
And another
And another . . .

Until the front yard
was nothing but

a pock-marked mess
of wet Alabama clay.

And as they sat exhausted,
damp, and discouraged,
they began to giggle
and then to laugh out loud
at how stupid they had been

To think that it would be
that easy to shuffle off
their destiny.

Rocking Chairs

On the front porch of the home place
the wind blew the
old oak rocking chairs
that Grandma and Grandpa
used to sit in and spin
those ghost tales
that kept us children spellbound.

As the rockers creaked in unison
my mind wandered back
to more innocent times
when kids really could believe
in spirits from the other side.

And then I realized
there was no wind.

Rocket to the Moon

When I was twelve
without a nickel to my name
I'd hang around the Greyhound station
and watch the buses
coming and going
like hissing, groaning dinosaurs
branded with mystical names
like Birmingham
and Memphis
and Jacksonville.

I'd watch the passengers
stepping off arriving buses
and wonder what exotic tales
they had to tell
of strange lands
like Atlanta
and Tupelo
and Panama City.

And then I'd watch each bus reload
with new riders
And as the Greyhound
grunted and moaned
and slowly rolled away
down a dark and rainy road
it was like watching the liftoff
of a rocket to the moon.

The Lowering of Ears

Babies haven't any hair;
Old men's heads are just as bare;
Between the cradle and the grave;
Lies a haircut and a shave.

— SAMUEL HOFFENSTEIN FROM *Songs*
of Faith in the Year after Next, VIII

I heard they put Jake the barber
in a nursing home today
and it brought back memories
of Jake's shop
where I had my first haircut
and my first flattop
and had my first ducktail trimmed
to just above my flipped-up collar.

Where once I saw George Wallace come in
for a trim and an oil change
smoking a smelly cigar
that simmered in one of the chrome ashtrays
on the counter
and fumigated the whole building.

The shop never changed.
Red vinyl barber chairs
with chrome arms
And green plastic waiting chairs

where at least three old men
were always sitting
reading the paper and
swapping lies
and spitting tobacco juice into wrinkled Dixie Cups.

Yellowed sketches on the wooden wall
of hairstyles from
generations long past.
The smell of cheap aftershave
and Wildroot Creme Oil
hung in the air
and calmed each customer
like some kind of barber incense.

The hypnotic snip—snip—snip
that always made me start to doze off
until my chin hit my chest
and woke me up
to look in the mirror
and see if Jake had skinned my head
while debating with some Auburn fan
about whether Bear Bryant was an alcoholic.

Dog-eared ancient magazines
and week-old newspapers strewn
across an worn out coffee table
that was brought in by Mrs. Jake
the only time I ever saw her
or any woman
in the shop.

It was a man's place
where old men warned young men
what life was all about and
shared their hard-learned wisdom.
Jake's Barber Shop is closed now.
Jake's son ran it for a while
before he got a civil service job at Maxwell
and sold the building to a pet store.

Last week I walked by
and peeked in at the bird cages
that sat where once old men
almost always misinformed me
about who was going to win the next election
except for picking Wallace every time
for governor
and that was no great feat.

Winos in the Sun

Against a warehouse wall
in the early morning sun
Sit two winos
laughing
and passing a pint between them.

Stuck in traffic
my blood pressure approaching stroke level
I creep toward a dreary job
that I hope to hold onto long enough

That someday
I'll be free
to sit against a warehouse wall
drinking wine
in the early morning sun.

Only the Good

I think it had gone past the point
of being envious or depressed,
because I knew that no one would
expect me to be that good.

— Eric Clapton's comment on a
performance by Stevie Ray Vaughn

One night I turned on
Austin City Limits
to see the Fabulous Thunderbirds
and the opening act was
Stevie Ray Vaughn
and he was singing Pride and Joy
and I couldn't believe
what I was hearing.

I said
Who the hell is that
and had that same feeling
I had when I first heard
Hound Dog
on my Aunt Vera's record player
and played it twenty-eight times
in a row.

And the first time I heard
Janis sing Ball and Chain
and sat in front of the TV
and almost cried.

And the first time I heard
Hendrix play Purple Haze
and wondered what planet
he was from.

And the first time I heard
the Doors do Light My Fire
and had to stop the car
and get out
and let it soak in.

Stevie Ray is long gone now
but not the ripples
in his pond.

Shadowboxing with Ginsberg

His thoughts were aching
Atrophied and cramped
As he strove to wax profound
by pliance
compliance
reliance upon
faux angst
that was merely
shadowboxing.

His poetry
distant echoes
of greater minds.
His light
a dim reflection
of their glow.

Frail young face
above frayed black turtleneck
Anemic beard
searching for form
He stood unsteady at the podium
upon which the great had lain
their immortality.

Appearing unaffected by it all
His cool
a mere absence
of heat.

From crumpled
yellow pages
lined in blue
He read.
Through
dead allusions
and wounded metaphors,
He read

Hoping that somewhere
in the far reaches
of his recitation
there would be
if not the sound of genius ringing
at least
a jingle
a slight metallic tingle . . .

But as he closed
and walked away
The spotlight slowly
died upon the stage
till there was
nothing left
but shadows.

Acid in the Park—1968

Lysergic acid diethylamide:
A drug used to induce
artificial schizophrenia.

Schizophrenia:
The state of believing that
you can change the world
by growing hair.

Life in the Key of C

Put your sweet lips a little closer to the phone and let's pretend that we're together all alone . . .

— JIM REEVES

I've always believed that
beer should be drunk in the key of C
Because that's the key that
the universe hums
And the best key
for singing
He'll Have to Go.

The Happy Time Bar & Grille

I could barely make out the shape
of small square tables
in the dim light from the beer signs
on the wall behind the bar.

There was the slight smell of
stale beer and pickles
in the smoky air.

As my eyes adjusted
I saw shadows
of desperation and despair
in the faces of the men
and boredom
in the glances of the women.

Bilson

Bilson was like a human snail
leaving a trail of slime
everywhere he went—
not really slime
but the essence of sliminess.

He had a look about him that inspired spite
from people who had never met him
And when he smiled
his smarmy smile
his eyes were dead and cold
and people looked away.

He had the handshake
of a corpse and the laugh of
a Halloween haunted house
that made people nervous
and uncomfortable.

Then one day a coked-out thug
came into the Zippy Mart
waving a forty-five
and Bilson stepped in
just in time to grab the gun
and take the bullet
meant for the lady clerk.
People who never laughed
at his jokes
wept at his funeral.

Doors

As we leave the rooms of experience
the doors of life close behind us
sometimes softly
sometimes quickly
sometimes slamming us in the ass.

PART III—
REALITIES

The days of our lives are threescore and ten; and if by reason of strength they be fourscore years, yet it is their strength labor and sorrow; for it is soon cut off, and we fly away.

— Psalms 90:10

A Beatnik State of Mind

*The Beat Generation, that was a vision that
we had, John Clellon Holmes and I, and Allen
Ginsberg,in an even wilder way . . . of a genera-
tion of crazy, illuminated hipsters suddenly rising
and roaming America, serious, curious, bumming
and hitchhiking everywhere, ragged, beatific,
beautiful in an ugly graceful new way . . . down
and out but of intense conviction.*

                       — JACK KEROUAC

I sit here in a beatnik state of mind
and fancy myself a poet
with something profound
yet hip
to tell the masses.

Bongo rhythms from years ago
echo in my head
pungent memories of pot smoke hang thick
in the dark basement of my brain
and I am once again deceived into mistaking
despair for enlightenment.

Shades of Black
and White and Gray

*The bonds that unite another person to ourself
exist only in our mind. Memory as it grows fainter
relaxes them, and notwithstanding the illusion by
which we would fain be cheated and with which,
out of love, friendship, politeness, deference, duty,
we cheat other people, we exist alone . . .*

— MARCEL PROUST

Spread out around the Formica table top
in my mother's little kitchen
are family photographs
of many decades.
Some I recognize
and some of friends and relatives
of whom I have only
a fuzzy recollection.

The funny thing about family photographs
is that they're not just images.
They're memory ships
that take us back to times and places
where everything was different.
Some things better—some worse.
Some innocent—some not so much
but still worth revisiting every now and then.

Someone told me that
you can never know where you are
or where you're going
without knowing where you've been.
And I as hold, one at a time,
these wrinkled pictures of a younger me
each one tells me its story
or maybe a fairy tale created in my head.

The pictures that are best (and worst) of all
are those of friends and family now passed
for whom there is no now—only then.
Freeze-framed in a four by five
forever smiling,
forever a part of each of us
who sit around the Formica table top
in my mother's little kitchen.

For Pop and Me

I was with Pop
when he died.
Not big to begin with,
he lay shrunken and shriveled
from cancer
under a pile of hospital blankets
that couldn't keep away the chill.

Bruce and Danny
had just left the room
when I reached to clutch
the hand
that he was trying to
lift from the bed.

And as I held his hand
his chest began to heave
and there was a gurgle in his throat
as he took his last breath.

And for just an instant
I thought of ringing for a nurse,
But no.
I wanted this moment
for just Pop and me.

I Went to Visit
Pop's Grave Today

I went to visit Pop's grave today
for the first time since
the funeral
seventeen years ago.

I can't remember
anything
about the funeral.
It's just a blur.

I can't even remember
If I cried.
I don't cry now.
But I want to.

Grandma's House

I had not seen Grandma's house
for many years
But I was still surprised to see
what was once the porch
piled high in the front yard
And I could tell that it wouldn't be long
before the house would be
completely gone.

The house where my infant footprints
still faintly show in the
the lumpy concrete walkway
that was poured by Grandpa
so long ago.

The house where we would spend
each holiday
sharing family meals
followed by drinking and dancing
to my brothers and I
playing raucously in the living room
where furniture was pulled back
against the wall
to make room for drums and amps.

And the noise would permeate
the neighborhood
until the cops knocked on the front door
which was our signal to

start the all-night poker game
on the dining room table
where Grandma would cuss like a sailor
and throw her cards
when three of a kind
beat her aces.

As I stood staring
at the remnants of the front porch
I couldn't help wondering
if somewhere among
the boards and bricks
were the Christmas lights
that Grandma always left strung up
all year long.

Unknown Rebel Soldier No. 12

As I walk the gravel graveyard path
among the many markers
of unknown Confederate dead
one softly calls my name
as though he knows me.

And as I kneel beside Unknown No. 12
I sense the presence of a skinny farm boy
barely twenty
married only weeks
when duty called him
to a hopeless war.

In a ragged brigade
of unhewn youth
he'd fought with honor many times
before being struck down
in a muddy field
by artillery from afar.

I sense that when he died
the war was lost already
and that he died with
his hand upon the Bible
in his pocket
and his young wife's name
upon his lips.

To Study God

God is a sea of infinite substance.

— St. John of Damascus

To study God
by hearing
one religion

Is to study music
by hearing
one song.

A Not So Beautiful Mind

I saw him sinking
into the damp black hole
of his madness
and there was nothing I could do.

At first it was funny when he said
those goofy things
and stapled his socks to the wall
instead of washing them.

But then he got to where
he heard voices
and cried for days
for no reason in particular.

And then for just a little while
he was Christ
and went around forgiving sins
and trying to heal the sick
and give the blind back their sight.

But then came that day
when he vacated the premises
of his mind
and hid in the basement
with his wrists caked in dried blood
and almost starved.

And the ambulance came
and took his shell away
to some red brick institution
where they keep his body alive.

For a time I would visit him
in that big room
with tile floors
and plastic chairs.

But the fog hung just too heavy
over the mind
that had put so many of our memories
in some dusty corner
that may never be reached again.

I saw him sinking
into the damp black hole
of his madness
and there was nothing I could do.

On Winning

*Victorious warriors win first and then go to war,
while defeated warriors go to war first and then
seek to win.*

— SUN-TZU

Winning is not about
how much you want to win
Or how much you hate to lose.
It's about how willing you are
to do what winners do.

Touchdown

For many years
I had not seen Dalraida Park.
so when I drove by today
I had to stop
and step again on the grass
where I scored my first touchdown
as a right halfback for Goode Street School
in the City Recreation League.

I stand on the spot
where Doug Goodwin
handed off the ball
for an off-tackle run
that turned into a sweep
when the hole was filled
by a pile of pudgy linemen
and an alert John Lloyd
body-blocked their linebacker
and opened up a path for me
to run eighty yards.

I stare at where the goal post used to be
and wonder how many other little boys
knew that same feeling
in that same end zone.

Randy Died Alone Last Week

They told me
Randy died alone last week
somewhere in California.
His heart gave out.
Just twenty-six.

I thought of
all the crazy things we'd done
and almost smiled.

Like the time we
hitchhiked home
from Panama City
Got picked up by a farmer
and wound up sleeping in a barn
to be awakened the next morning
by two curious cows.

And when we found out
that Richard was the desk clerk
at a whorehouse
near the train station
and took advantage
of the situation.

And then there was the day
that Randy opened his locker
to show me
the loaded thirty-eight

he'd later use
to terrorize
a high school bully.

Then came the day he said
he was leaving
to follow his dream and
be the first in his family
to make something of himself.

They told me
Randy died alone last week
somewhere in California.

Broken Parole

You
BROKE PAROLE
By hanging with
KNOWN FELONS.
(They're a baaad influence.)

You're
REVOKED.
No more parole for you.
You know you can't hang with
KNOWN FELONS.
(They're a baaad influence.)

It's
NO JOKE.
No more parole.
You can't hang with
KNOWN FELONS.
(They're a baaad influence.)

You
BROKE PAROLE
So now you're back in
POKE
with all those other
PAROLE BREAKERS
and
KNOWN FELONS.

Execution at Parchman

He that smiteth a man, so that he die,
Shall he be surely put to death.

— GENESIS 21:12

The moon was crying
in the Delta night.
A hoot owl moaning low.

A bobcat's wail
rode the midnight wind
through drizzle on death row.

His hands were trembling
against his lips
when he heard the death bell toll

As he softly prayed
one final time
for God to save his soul.

A southbound freight
went rumbling by.
Its whistle moaning low.

His mother's wail
rode the midnight wind
through drizzle on death row.

His hands were trembling
against his hips
when he heard the death bell toll

As he slowly walked
that final mile
to where he'd lose his soul.

Egg Self-Actualized

A plain boiled egg
white and bland
dipped in boiling colors
stuck with a rabbit decal
becomes a treasure
to be hidden in the grass.

Why Is It?

Why is it that
just as I have to stop drinking
the City approves draft beer sales?
I love draft beer.
It's so cold
and foamy
and good.

And why is it that
just as I get married
the City approves nudie bars?
I love nudie bars.
They're so hot
and naughty
and fun.

And why is it that
just as I trade my Vette for a van
the City builds a drag strip?
I love drag strips.
They're so cool
and exciting
and loud.

And why is it that
just as I swear off gambling
the City approves a casino?
I love casinos.
They're so bright

and jingly
and weird.

And why is it that
I haven't already left
this damn city
before they do something else right.

What's the Word?

In the beginning was the Word, and the Word was
with God, and the Word was God.

— St. John 1:1

The Word was God
And the Word was Jesus.
And Hitler was the Word
And Mao.

And Bob Dylan was the Word.
And Dylan Thomas
And Lenny Bruce
And Harper Lee.

And Lennon was the Word.
And Lenin was the Word.

And Shakespeare was the Word.
And Arthur Miller.
And Woody Allen.

And Cosmo was the Word.
And Playboy.
And the National Enquirer.

And Muhammad was the Word.
And Gandhi
And Alice Cooper.

And Hank Williams was the Word.
And Elvis
And Darth Vader.

And Richard Pryor was the Word.
And Robert Johnson
And Brother Dave Gardner.

And Hemingway was the Word.
And Fitzgerald
And Jonathan Livingston Seagull.

Walter Cronkite was the Word.
And David Brinkley
And Jay Leno.

And the bird, bird, bird
The bird is the Word.

And the Word was with God,
And the Word was God.

Let Me Have Back Those Days

Let me have back those days
when I could feel the sun
and smell the flowers
and the rain.

When every touch was new
and my heart beat hard
and sometimes there were reasons to laugh or cry.

When I could taste wine
and bread
and the love on your mouth.

When getting old
was something
other people did.

Politics

Politics appears to soil the soul
as surely as
the pure white early morning snow
will always turn into brown mush
on the street.

Blue Words on a
Yellow Legal Pad

As I scribble words onto a yellow legal pad
I am intrigued by the shape of my ideas.
Not their substance, mind you,
there's very little of that,
but the images they form on the page

Blue squiggly lines that go up and down
and across
and then up and down and across again
Smeared and crossed through
with arrows and circles here and there
and every once in a while a box
imprisoning a word or two
to remind me that I can do better.

Almost illegible markings
even to me.
But no matter
I don't have much to say anyway.

Last Laugh Haiku

Hiroshima
Nagasaki
Karaoke.

About the Author

ED GEORGE, of Prattville, Alabama, is an attorney
and education management consultant who likes
to try his hand at songwriting, poetry, and painting
when he's not playing softball or tennis. This is his
third collection of poetry.